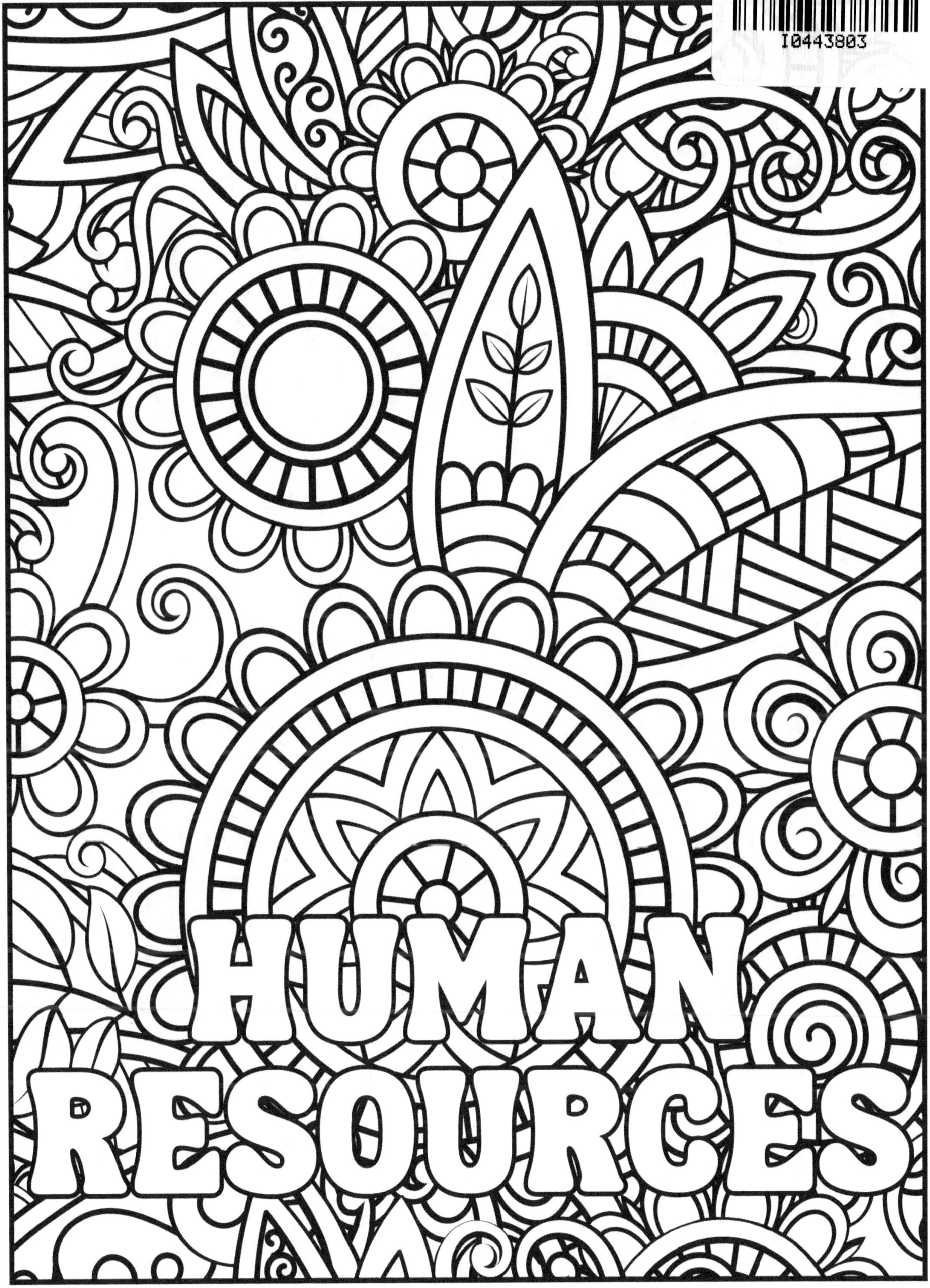
HUMAN
RESOURCES

KEEP UP THE
GOOD
WORK

But
FIRST
COFFEE

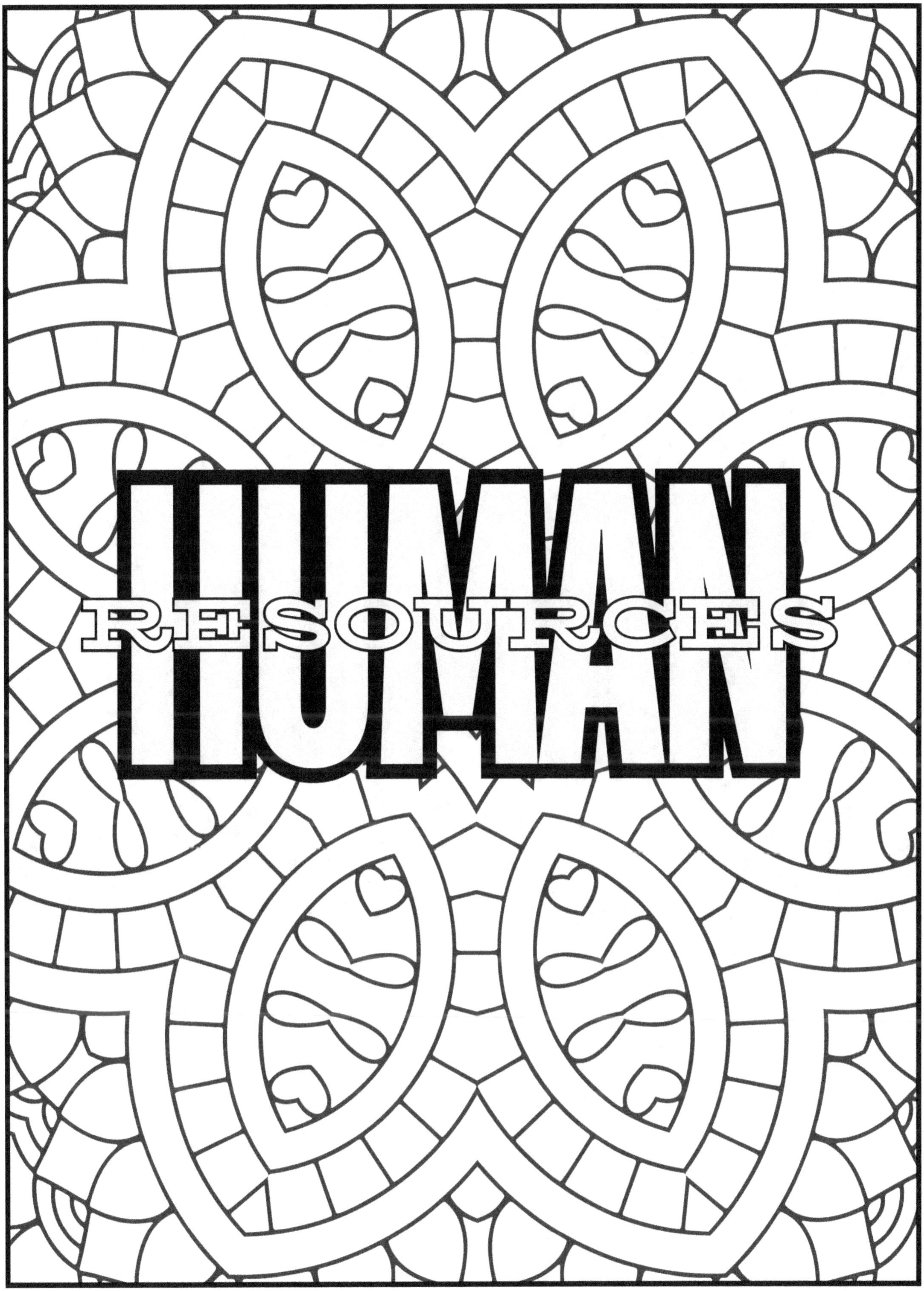
HUMAN
RESOURCES

DON'T MAKE
ME USE MY
HR
VOICE

But did
you
document
it?

HR
QUEEN

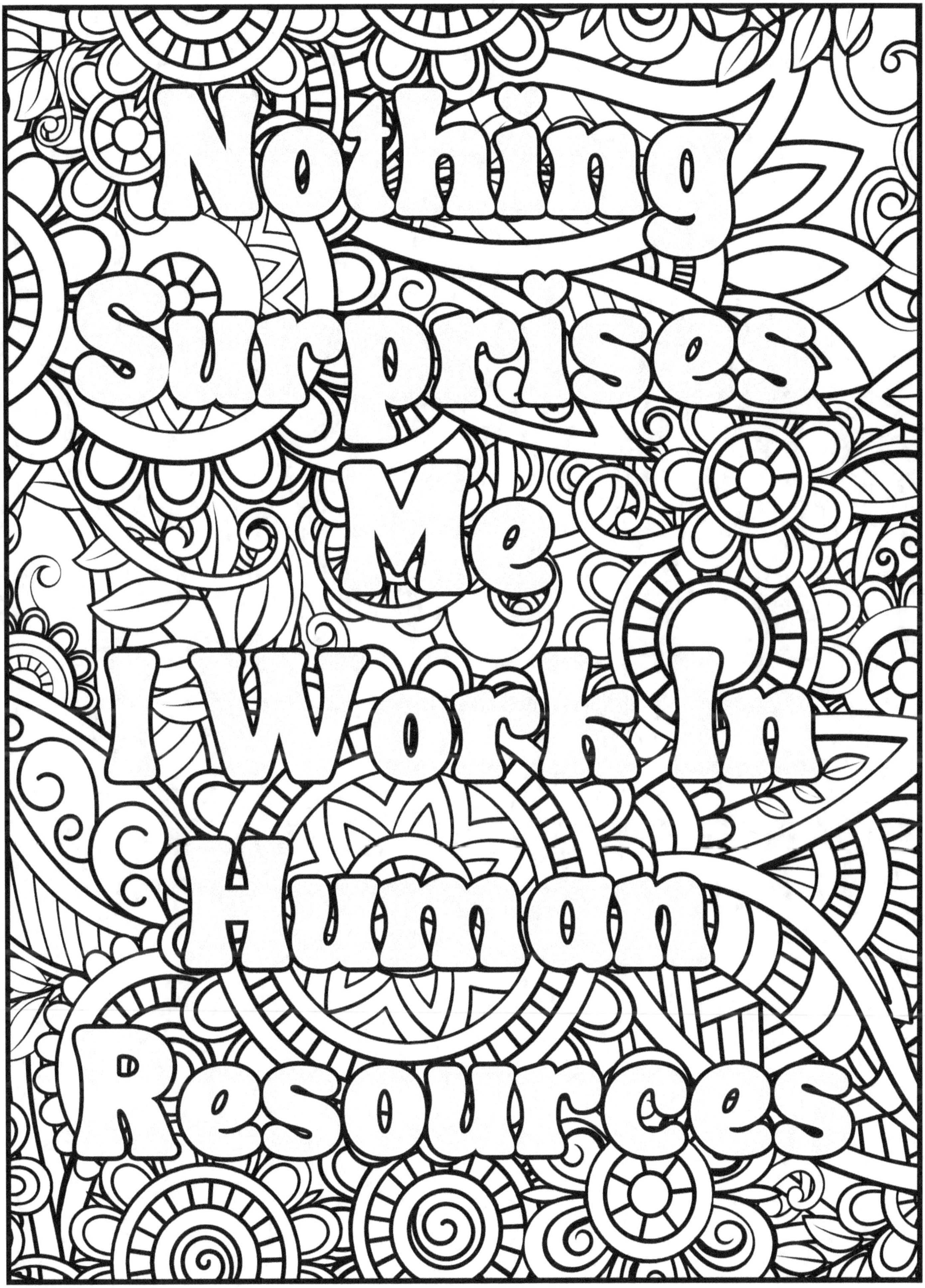
Nothing Surprises Me I Work In Human Resources

What Happens In
HR
Stays in
HR

HR

HR
SQUAD

YOU CAN'T
Spell
HERO
Without
"HR"

Live
what you
Love

Girl Boss

LIVE YOUR
PURPOSE

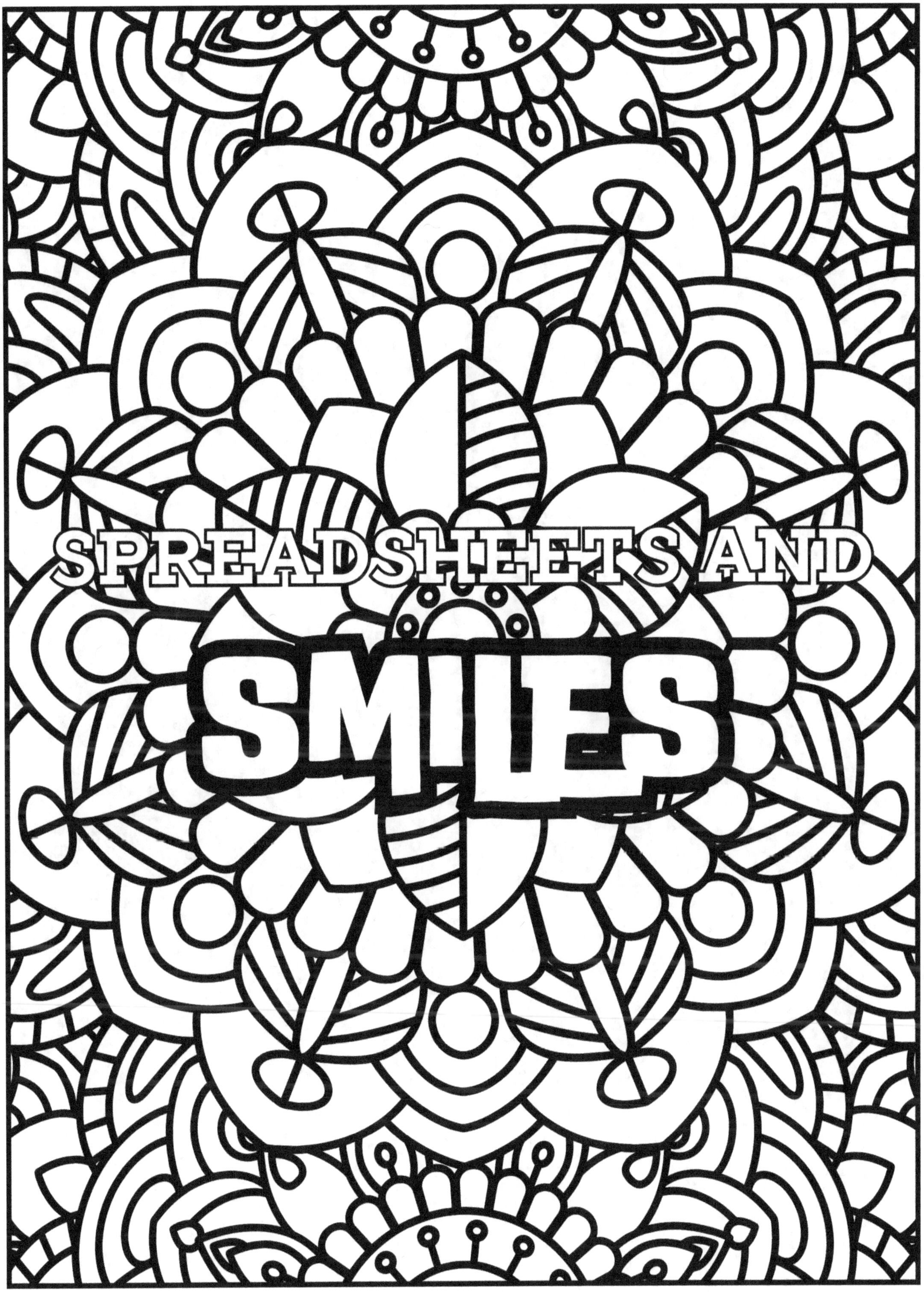
SPREADSHEETS AND
SMILES

LEADERSHIP
WHISPERER

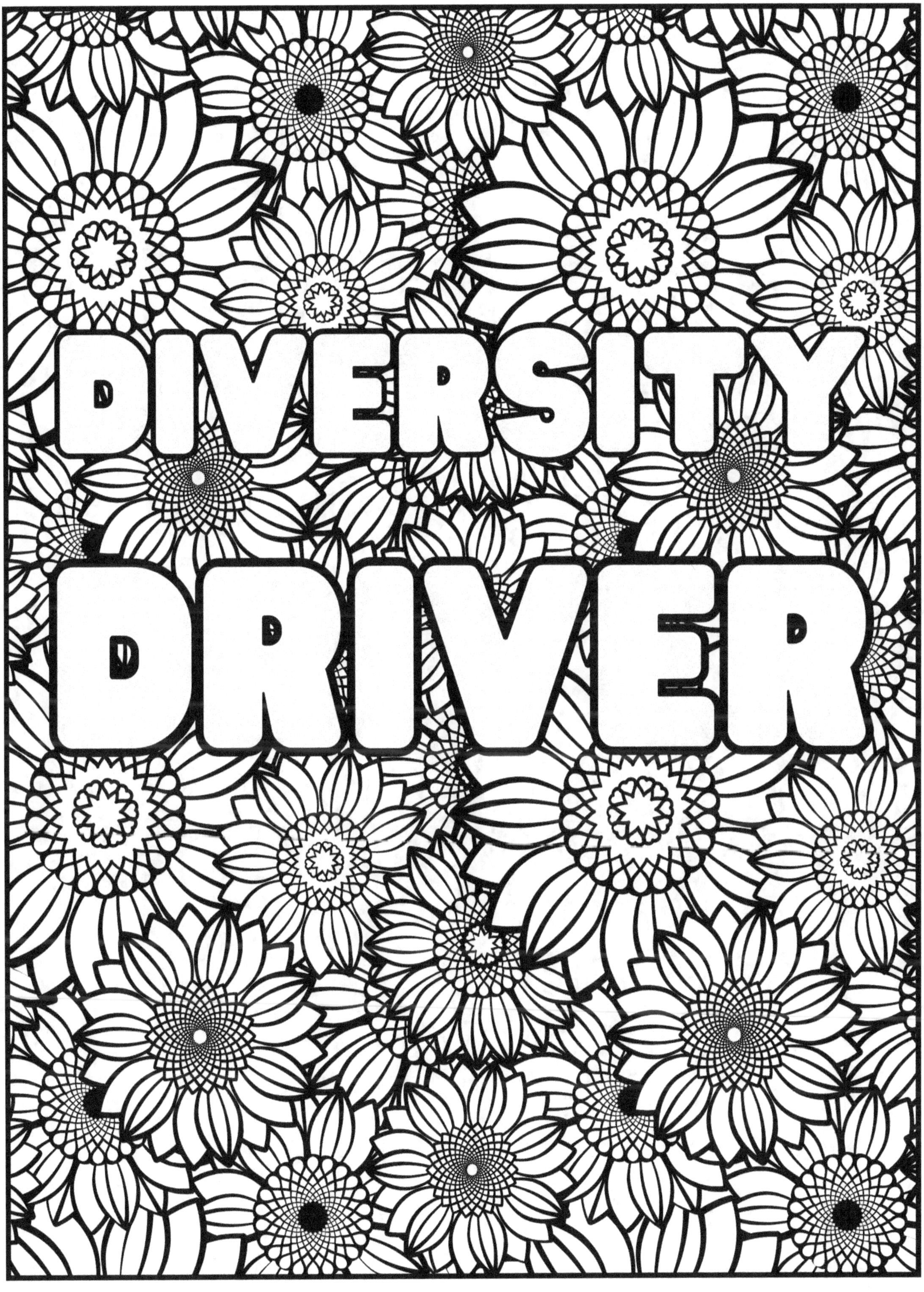
DIVERSITY
DRIVER

I can
&
I will

WAKE
UP &
SLAY

TAKE
the
RISK

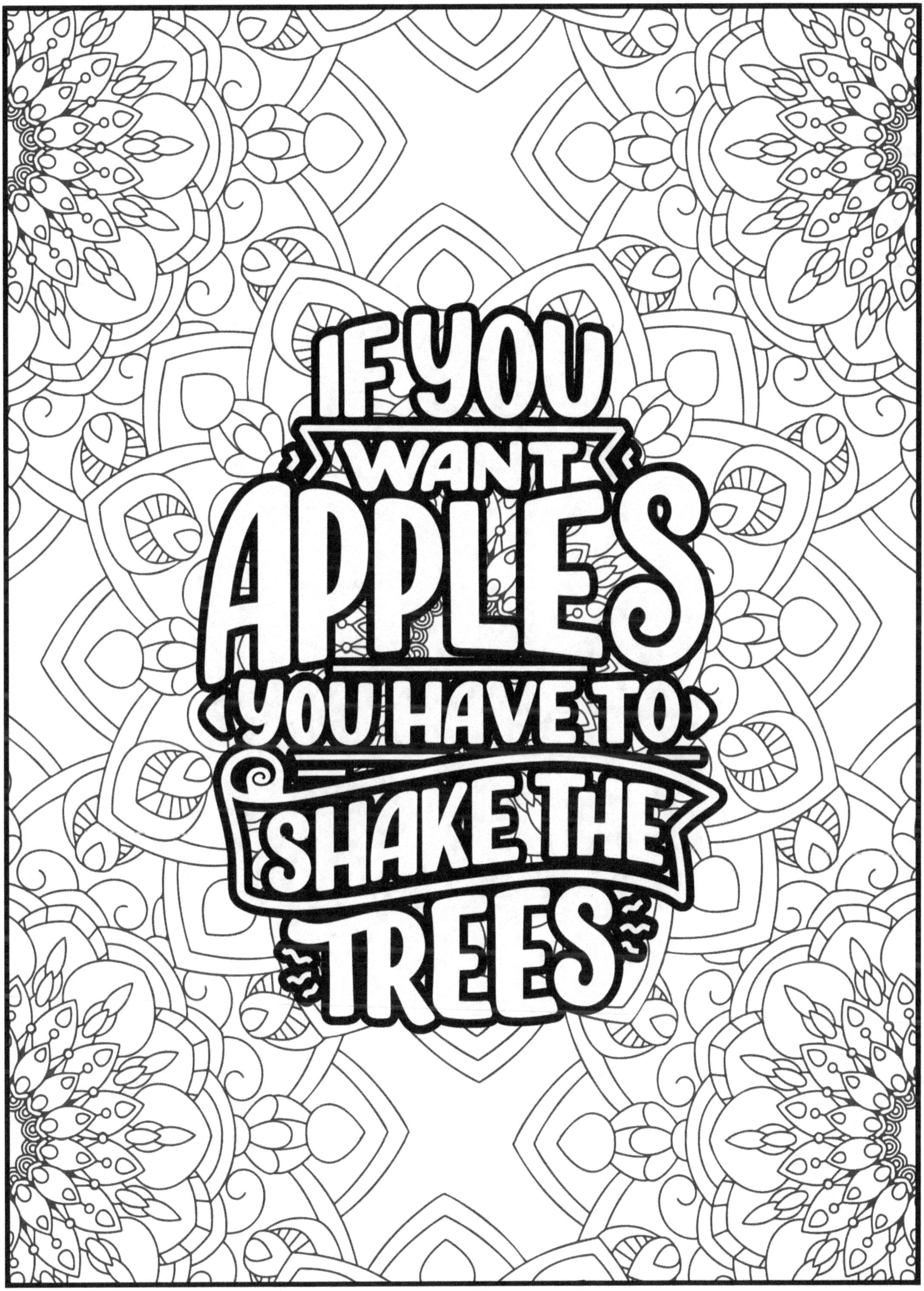
IF YOU
WANT
APPLES
YOU HAVE TO
SHAKE THE
TREES

Just A
Girl
With
Goals

learn
SOMETHING
- new -
EVERYDAY

BE
Fearless

Think
POSITIVE

TREAT
yourself

DON'T STOP
until
you're
PROUD

START NOW

Life
IS
TOUGH
BUT
SO
are
you

www.ingramcontent.com/pod-product-compliance
Lightning Source LLC
Chambersburg PA
CBHW082219220526
45470CB00010B/3238
* 9 7 9 8 3 2 4 8 4 1 0 4 1 *